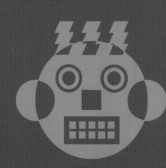

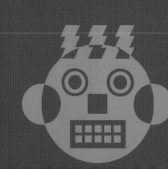

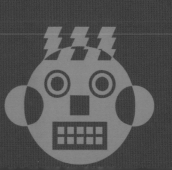

LET THERE BE LIFE!

Animating with the Computer

Christopher W. Baker

Walker and Company
New York

To my wife, Melissa, and my son, Elliott,
two loves who make it all worthwhile.

A note regarding the art in this book: Computer imagery created for video is produced at resolutions
adequate for that medium. When printed, however, these images can lose clarity.

First published in the United States of America in 1997 by

Walker Publishing Company, Inc.

Published simultaneously in Canada by Thomas Allen & Son Canada, Limited, Markham, Ontario

Library of Congress Cataloging-in-Publication Data
Baker, Christopher W.
Let there be life!: animating with the computer/Christopher W. Baker.
p.   cm.
Includes index.
Summary: Explains how the computer is used to create animation and compares
the approach to traditional animation.
ISBN 0-8027-8472-0 (hc). —ISBN 0-8027-8473-9 (rein.)
1. Computer animation—Juvenile literature. [1. Computer animation.] I. Title.
TR897.7.B343   1997
778.5′347′028566—dc20   96-23289
CIP
AC

Book design by Janice Noto-Helmers

Printed in Hong Kong

2 4 6 8 10 9 7 5 3 1

Welcome to the World of Animation

A giant red sun hangs above the waters on an alien planet. *(Courtesy of MetaTools Software.)*

Imagine a world, a physical world you can touch and see. It is a world of sprawling cities with towering skyscrapers, as well as farms and country homes with manicured lawns and gardens. It is a world much like your own, except for one thing: It is completely under your control.

At your whim, an eerie orange glow bathes a planet's surface as its giant red sun rises above the horizon. The sky flares from its deep nighttime blue to a fiery red. For the second time in six months, the Zorg from Alpha Centauri has broken its restraints at the Interplanetary Zoo and is roaming the city. Smoke billows from the remains of a shattered building. A solitary alien cry echoes above the corridors of the frightened metropolis. . . .

In the world of computer animation, the only limit is your imagination. Today, almost anything you can see or imagine can be pictured on the computer screen. This new power to create lifelike pictures out of nothing but the computer is changing what we see on television and in the movie theater.

Animating the Old-Fashioned Way

Walt Disney is recognized as the father of traditional animation. Back in the 1920s he made his first animated short film, *Steamboat Willy*, which introduced the now famous Mickey Mouse. This was well before anyone had even begun to think about electronic computers. In fact, computers did not begin to play a major part in animation until the 1980s. Before that almost all animations were created by hand, one frame at a time.

This traditional form of hand animation is called *cel animation*. A cel is a sheet of clear plastic on which an artist draws a single picture. To make a film in the old days, animators drew long series of such pictures, changing each image slightly from the one before it. As you might guess, cel animation was a lot of work. Disney's first feature-length animation, *Snow White*, took more than three years to produce, requiring over 119,500 separate cels.

You can get a feel for the process of cel animation by creating a flip book. First, take several small sheets of paper and staple them together along one edge. Then begin to draw your cels. Stick figures work just fine; simply make each drawing slightly different from the previous one. When you have completed the series, flip the pages with your thumb and watch the action.

Facing page: Chrome reptiles wander over a barren landscape of another world.

Bringing Animation into the Future

For over fifty years, anyone who wished to create an animated cartoon or film had to do it by hand. In the early 1960s, however, Ivan Sutherland, a young Ph.D. student at MIT, taught a computer how to draw.

The computer he used was huge, filling an entire room and costing millions of dollars, and his drawing was primitive: only straight lines, circles, and a few very basic geometric shapes like cubes and spheres. These crude beginnings, however, launched an entire industry.

During these early days of *computer graphics*, as this new science was called, creating pictures was extremely difficult. For each image they wanted to create, early computer graphics researchers had to write complex software programs that often took many hours to run before they saw any results. Programming errors—and there were plenty—meant the whole process had to be repeated over and over. In fact, a single picture could take days to create. In the early days of computer animation, drawing an image by hand was far easier than creating it by computer.

Today animators work at computer terminals and see the results of their efforts on a monitor. *(Courtesy of Pacific Data Images.)*

One major problem for early computer animators: There were no easy-to-use PCs or Macintosh computers. Computers then cost hundreds of thousands of dollars, if not millions, and some were so large they filled entire buildings. Yet, they had far less processing power than today's two-hundred-dollar, handheld Nintendo game machines.

ortunately those days are a thing of the past. Even though the most advanced computer animations can still require huge amounts of software programming, there are few animations today that are created without the aid of the computer. Virtually every special-effects and animation studio, from the extensive facilities at filmmaker George Lucas's Industrial Light & Magic to the one- and two-person studios that are popping up across the country, uses computers to create its work.

ot only has the computer made the animation process more efficient, but it has also added a new dimension for artists to explore. If you look closely at traditional animation, you will notice that everything looks flat. This is because there is no depth to the images. Early animators like Disney knew that adding a realistic third dimension would greatly increase the complexity of any drawing and make the creation of animated feature films an impossible dream. The computer, however, provides this third dimension, and much more, essentially for free.

Just what do we mean when we talk about a third dimension in animation? Take a look around. Everything that exists in your world not only has height and width but also has depth. A book, a table, a favorite pet, your best friend—they all have three dimensions: We can walk around them; they cast shadows; they look small when they are far away and larger up close.

Graphic tools make the whole process of creating imaginary worlds easier to understand. *(Courtesy of MetaTools Software.)*

Traditional cel animation tries to imitate these qualities in a comical sort of way by using crude, flat backgrounds across which the characters move. Computer animation, however, through complex mathematical calculations, can replicate these qualities exactly, with no additional effort on the part of the artist. Thus objects and characters in computer animations appear to have solidity and substance. They can be viewed from any angle, top to bottom, as well as up close or from a distance. The software and the hardware automatically create the needed sense of perspective.

The process of creating a computer animation begins with a story. This is usually described in a storyboard—a series of rough, hand-drawn sketches that look much like the Sunday newspaper funnies. Each box shows an important scene in the story. Surprisingly enough, even today most storyboards are still drawn with pencil on paper.

It is the storyboard that gives the director and the animators a visual reference from which they work. From the storyboard they can see what the characters will look like, get a rough idea of the sets, and understand how the action will evolve.

A portion of the storyboard for *Arnie & Birnie*, a short film about a dog and a flea. *(Courtesy of Windlight Studios.)*

Facing page: The baby from Pixar's film *Tin Toy* plays merrily in his imaginary living room. Note the feeling of depth here and compare it against the flat look of your favorite newspaper comic strip. *(© 1988 Pixar. All rights reserved.)*

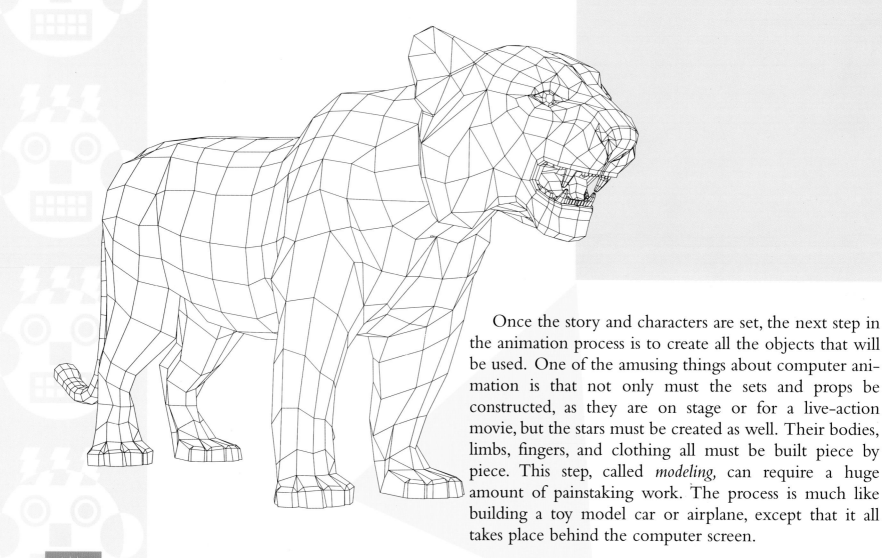

This low-resolution wireframe model of a tiger is ready to be animated and colored. *(Courtesy of Viewpoint DataLabs.)*

Once the story and characters are set, the next step in the animation process is to create all the objects that will be used. One of the amusing things about computer animation is that not only must the sets and props be constructed, as they are on stage or for a live-action movie, but the stars must be created as well. Their bodies, limbs, fingers, and clothing all must be built piece by piece. This step, called *modeling,* can require a huge amount of painstaking work. The process is much like building a toy model car or airplane, except that it all takes place behind the computer screen.

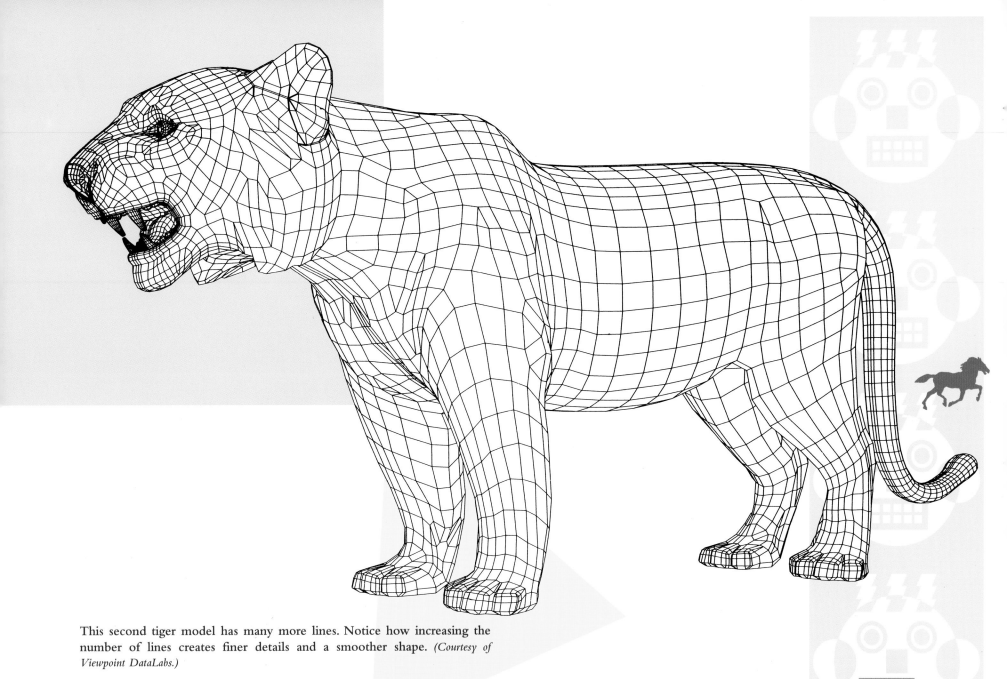

This second tiger model has many more lines. Notice how increasing the number of lines creates finer details and a smoother shape. *(Courtesy of Viewpoint DataLabs.)*

Making a Model

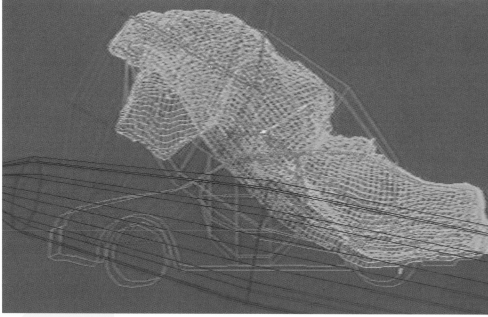

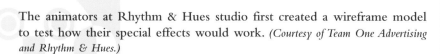
The animators at Rhythm & Hues studio first created a wireframe model to test how their special effects would work. *(Courtesy of Team One Advertising and Rhythm & Hues.)*

There are several approaches to building a computer model. The first, and most common, is to start with a blank screen and use the graphics software to build the object line by line. In this case, the computer supplies a three-dimensional space within which the modeler creates the object by clicking and dragging lines into place.

Since the model being built is three-dimensional, it can be rotated and moved on the screen, and worked on from any angle. If you are constructing a circular table, for example, you might first draw the round top and add thickness to it. Next you could create the legs, flipping the tabletop upside down to attach them at precisely the right spots. You could then turn the entire object back over, and your table would be ready for use.

The only problem is that the model doesn't yet look like any table you ever saw. It has no solid-looking surfaces and is made up of only a series of lines that outline its shape. This is called a *wireframe representation* because it looks as if someone has taken a bendable wire and wrapped it around the outside of the table. In between the lines the table is transparent. If it were standing on top of an oriental rug, you would be able to see through to the carpet beneath it. The use of a wireframe representation saves computer time and makes it easier to reuse a model for a different task. Generally, it is not until farther along in the animation process that an object gets a solid surface.

Here is the same image after animation and rendering were completed. *(Courtesy of Team One Advertising and Rhythm & Hues.)*

13

Automatic Modeling

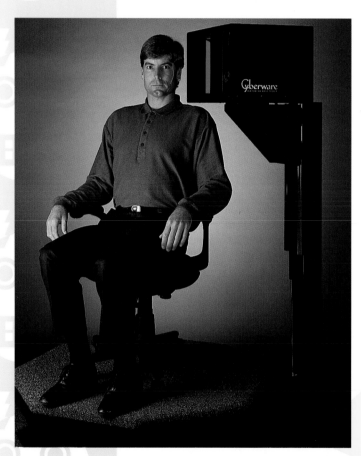

The red light on the actor's cheek is a laser beam that is rapidly scanning the shape of his face. *(Courtesy of Cyberware.)*

In some cases, the model you need to build is so complex or irregularly shaped that creating it line by line would take too much time. The human face, for example, has many subtle curves and lines that make each face distinct. Copying these curves and lines manually is simply too difficult for the human animator to manage.

Similarly, highly detailed models with odd surface shapes, such as might be found on an alien spacecraft, could take too long for the modeler to build from scratch. In these cases, modelers often turn to a relatively new piece of hardware, called a *3-D scanner*, to do the job.

There are two basic types of scanners, one of which uses a laser beam and the other a magnetic field. For a laser-based system to scan a human face, a person has to sit absolutely still while a low-powered laser moves rapidly over his or her features. The process lasts only a matter of minutes. For the laser to scan a spacecraft, a physical model has to be built first and then placed in the scanner. In either case, the process results in the creation of a highly detailed wireframe model that can then be further refined, and later animated, inside the computer.

This first-of-its-kind laser scanner is large enough to scan an entire human body. *(Courtesy of Cyberware.)*

From an earlier scan, the computer has built a detailed wireframe model of a woman's head. *(Courtesy of Cyberware.)*

Magnetic scanners produce the same result, but in a slightly different manner. The object to be scanned, the spaceship model for example, is first covered with a grid of thin black tape. The model is then placed inside a strong magnetic field. There, each of the intersections of the tape grid are manually touched with a magnetic pen. The computer calculates the position of these points and builds the final wireframe model.

Sculptor Diana Walczak places a fine tape grid on her sculpture of Michael Jackson for his *HIStory* video. *(Courtesy of Kleiser-Walczak Construction Company © 1995.)*

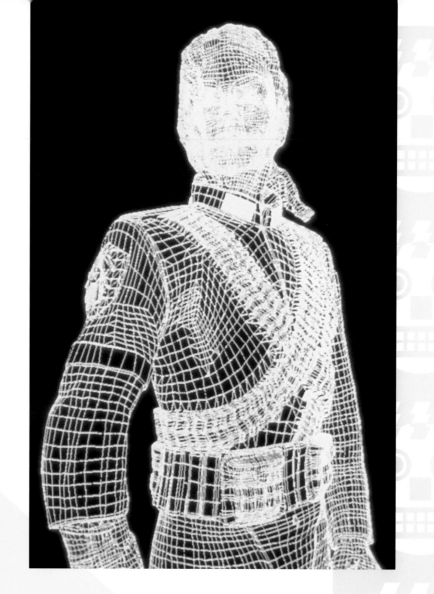

Here we see the finished Jackson sculpture (left) completely covered with the scanning grids. From the grid, the computer has built a highly detailed three-dimensional model (right) that is now ready to be animated. *(Courtesy of Kleiser-Walczak Construction Company © 1995.)*

Using the Library

third way to build models is to use the library. No, not the local public library. The libraries that modelers use are either those assembled by the studio at which they work or those produced by commercial companies that specialize in creating computer models.

For example, if a studio has previously completed a TV commercial for an automobile company, and if that company asks the studio to do another, it can simply reuse the computer model created for the first commercial. This can save a tremendous amount of work because the modeler can simply call up the needed wireframe from the library. With other projects, the studio might simply purchase a ready-made model from a commercial modeler.

Facing page: Viewpoint DataLabs created this incredibly detailed termite. It is one of hundreds of three-dimensional models sold by the company. *(Courtesy of Viewpoint DataLabs.)*

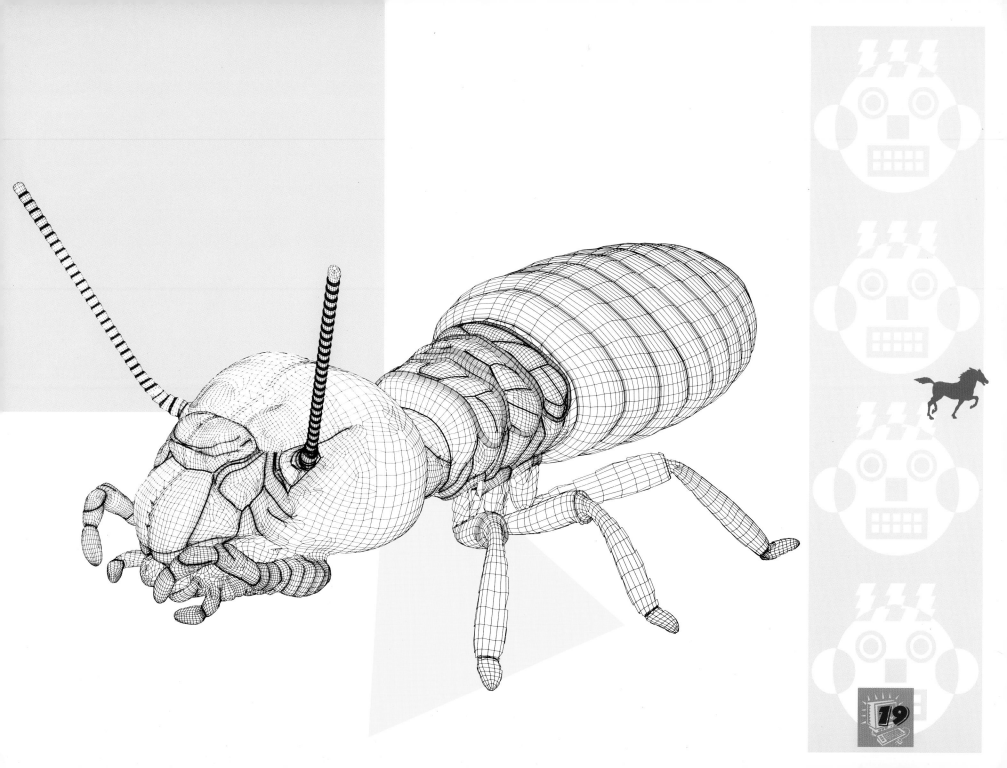

Bringing the Story to Life

For the short film *Locomotion*, every part of the train, tracks, and tunnel first had to be modeled before the animators could bring the train to life. *(© 1986 Pacific Data Images. All rights reserved.)*

With the modeling step complete and all the sets, props, and characters constructed, we are ready to bring the story to life. This is the heart of the animation process. Once again, the computer makes the process much easier than it used to be.

An animator can make a three-dimensional model do almost anything.
Here the train is pulling back in alarm at a break in the tracks ahead.

21

A sequence of four frames from Pixar's film *André and Wally B.* shows André pointing in one direction for the bee and running off the other way.

For one thing, with the computer controlling the dimensions of the characters, sets, and props, no variation in size can occur unless the animator intends for it to happen. A computer-animated Alice in Wonderland, for example, might change size across a series of frames after eating the cake or drinking the potion. But she wouldn't do so without the consent of the animator.

A second problem occurs when an error is made or the director wants to change the action. With traditional cel animation, errors and adjustments usually require that entire sequences, often dozens of frames long, be thrown away and redrawn. With the computer this problem does not arise.

It's not that computer animators make no mistakes or that modern animation directors avoid changes. These certainly occur in any production. When they do happen, however, they are far easier to repair. For example, if a director decides a cartoon would be funnier if the main character were fatter or had shorter arms, the animator can simply change the shape of the model and the computer would insert that change everywhere in the cartoon.

Similarly, changing the characters' movements is just as easy because the computer permits animators to break the animation down into its component parts. Each part's motion can then be adjusted separately until it is perfect, at which point the various parts can be put back together in finished form.

Hand-drawn cel animation presents several difficulties that are virtually eliminated by the computer. One problem is that it's extremely difficult to maintain the exact size of a hand-drawn figure across several cels. As an experiment, take two sheets of paper and draw exactly the same image on each sheet. Chances are, no matter how hard you try, there will be at least some slight differences, even if you trace it.

Making the Action Move

In the computer cartoon *The Incredible Crash Dummies*, the animators did just that. To animate the two star crash dummies, Slick and Spin, they created a hierarchy of movement, animating the largest elements, such as the heroes' bodies, first, and then working down to the finer details of their hands and feet.

They started by creating the path along which the dummies moved. As the characters entered Dr. Zub's lab, for example, their bodies bumped into walls, each other, and various props. Once the director was satisfied with this large-scale movement, the animators developed the actions of each dummy's legs and arms. As with the body movements, they animated the arms and legs using the computer mouse, clicking and dragging them to the desired places. Finally, after the arm and leg movements were approved, the animators added the more subtle hand, foot, and finger motions. You can see from this process that any mistakes made along the way can simply be isolated and reworked until the scene is perfect.

Facing page: Crash dummies Slick and Spin join Dr. Zub in his lab. (© 1993 Tyco Industries.)

Letting the Computer Help

Animators routinely use the computer to automatically move their characters in certain limited ways. Let's say, for example, that the animated toy in Pixar's Oscar-winning short film, *Tin Toy*, has to raise his hands to cover his eyes. The motion is simple and smooth. Why should the animator have to create every single frame of that motion by hand? If the software is sophisticated enough, the animator won't have to. He or she simply shows the computer where the beginning and ending positions of the hands are to be, tells it how many frames are needed, and the computer automatically moves the hands and creates the frames.

Even in scenes loaded with complex action, the computer can create one out of every two, or sometimes two out of every three, frames per sequence. When you consider that a ninety-minute animation has nearly 130,000 individual frames, you can see how this cuts the workload considerably.

As for letting the computer do more than these *in-between frames*, as they are called, it is currently both impossible and undesirable. What makes animation captivating is the personality the animator gives to the characters. This is done through quirks of movement, exaggerations, and other tricks that require a keen sense of humor. In other words, until the computer develops its own personality, complete with human emotions and sensitivities, the talent and creativity of the animator are of primary importance.

Facing page: Tinny, from Pixar's *Tin Toy*, smiles. Note the shadows, lighting, and depth that make Tinny's world seem real. (*© 1988 Pixar. All rights reserved.*)

27

Animating with Your Whole Body

Sitting at a terminal and moving the characters, part by part, is not the only way to animate. What if you wanted your characters to dance, or jump, or run, just like human beings. This is extremely difficult to do at the computer screen. The results almost always look fake.

To create more reality-based animations, *performance animation* has been developed. Performance animation captures the actual movements of a human actor by connecting him or her to a computer. An actor or performer first puts on special clothing with electronic sensors attached at key locations such as the wrists, elbows, shoulders, and hips. Wires run from these sensors to a computer.

Animator Joan Stavely, dressed in a performance animation suit, creates a dancing "motion file." *(Courtesy of Windlight Studios.)*

Facing page: Stavely's movements were later attached to a computer model for a doll in a test for an upcoming advertisement. *(Courtesy of Windlight Studios.)*

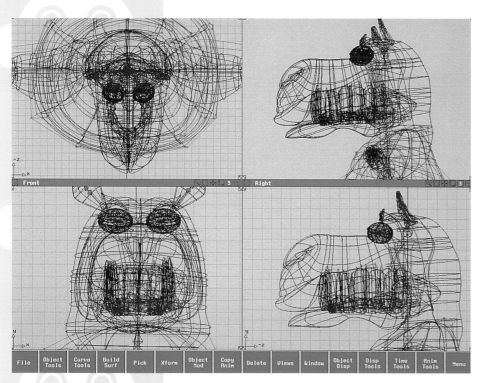

Wireframe images of a computer-generated character's head. *(Courtesy of Windlight Studios.)*

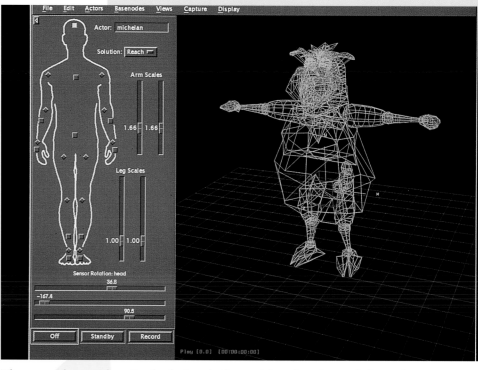

The same character's entire body, in wireframe (above), as it was being animated by performance animation, and the same character in solid form (facing page). *(Courtesy of Windlight Studios.)*

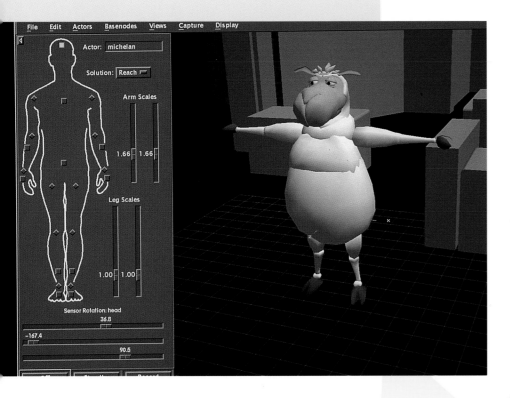

Because we are hu-man, and we see other humans every day, we are highly sensitive to the way people move. Thus in an animation, we immediately notice anything that does not fit the normal pattern of movement. Once this happens, we stop believing that the character is real, thereby weaken-ing the power of the movie to capture our imaginations.

The performer then steps into a strong magnetic field and goes through his or her act. The computer knows where each sensor is located inside the magnetic field at any given time, and from this knowledge builds up what is called a *motion file*. In many ways, the process is very sim-ilar to the automatic model building mentioned earlier, only a lot faster.

Two actors in performance animation gear cavort on stage to create the motion file for the dog Arnie in *Arnie & Birnie*. *(Courtesy of Windlight Studios.)*

Here is Arnie caught in one of his exaggerated strides from the previously created motion file. *(© 1995 Windlight Studios. All rights reserved.)*

Another way to capture movements is via high-speed cameras. This fencer is surrounded by six video cameras that track the white balls stuck to his body. There are no wires to get in the way. *(Courtesy of Motion Analysis.)*

The motion file can then be attached to a computer-generated character like Arnie the dog in Windlight Studios' short film *Arnie & Birnie*. In fact, this is precisely what was done. Two actors, one for Arnie's front legs and one for the back, put on the motion sensors and acted out just how Arnie moved.

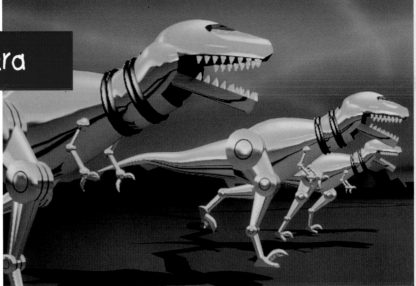

Imagine a set built for a live-action movie. It takes up space, and the director can position the camera anywhere within that space and even move the camera while the action takes place.

The exact same thing applies inside the computer. There are three-dimensional characters and sets, and there also is a camera. This camera can be positioned inside the computer set anywhere the director desires, and it will capture the action from that angle.

What's more, the computer camera has several advantages over a real movie camera. It is invisible, so it never gets in the way. And it has no weight, mass, or solidity. This means it can fly through the set on any path the director chooses while recording the action. It can even move through walls.

In the short film *Sleepy Guy*, the camera is positioned above and to the side of the man and his dog.

Facing page: Notice the camera change in these two stills from the short film *Chromosaurus*. Just as in live-action films, the computer camera can show the action close-up or farther away.

Looking Good

So far we have created computer models and made them come alive, but, as you might suspect, we still have more work to do. Now we must make everything look good. When we were discussing modeling, we mentioned that the table we created was built only in wireframe. Somehow we have to fill in the transparent holes and add color, shadows, and reflections, if necessary.

This all happens in the final step, called *rendering*. During the rendering phase, the computer creates all the visible surfaces of all the wireframe objects. It takes the colors and textures specified by the animators and then sticks them onto these surfaces like wallpaper.

The rendering software can even attach video footage to a specified surface, so the characters in a cartoon can watch the same TV shows we do!

Before rendering, Red, the unicycle from the film *Red's Dream*, is gray and lifeless. After rendering (facing page), Red not only has a bright coat of paint but has highlights and shadows to give him depth and dimension.

In addition to painting the objects with color and texture, shiny objects can be made to reflect the other computer-created elements that surround it. A computer-generated fishbowl full of water, for example, can reflect the animated room around it just the way a real fishbowl might reflect your family room.

The rendering step also includes the creation of shadows and the designing of specific lighting patterns. With animation software you can place lights anywhere you want and adjust their intensities as well as their colors. It is much like being on a real movie set.

Facing page: The details of the bicycle shop in *Red's Dream*—the spokes, the tire treads, the shadows, the light—would be almost impossible to produce without the computer.

Controlling the Scene

The similarity to the real world ends quickly, however. Imagine telling a real sofa not to cast a shadow and ordering the chair next to it to do so when the light comes on. In the computer world, just because an object appears solid, doesn't mean it has to cast a shadow. You can decide on exactly the look you want. A near perfect lighting environment can be designed through careful, but limited, use of computer-generated shadows.

Once all the lights, colors, textures, shadows, and reflections have been defined, it is time to send each of the frames to the renderer. The renderer is not a person but a software program. It calculates the final look of everything in each frame, based on what the animators and lighting designers have specified.

Top: Pacific Data Images first created the Pillsbury Doughboy in low resolution and without color. Note the indistinct edges on his body. *(Used with permission from Pillsbury.)*

Right: Here is the Doughboy after rendering. His body is now smooth and round, and his sleeves are brightly colored. *(Used with permission from Pillsbury.)*

Facing page: Finally, the computer-generated Doughboy is placed in the TV commercial next to a plate of cookies and a roll of dough. *(Used with permission from Pillsbury.)*

Rendering of the final, highly detailed images requires a massive number of mathematical calculations. With very complex scenes, even the most high-powered graphics computers can require several hours to produce the final frame. For this reason, finished frames are usually rendered overnight when the computers are not being used by the animators. The frames to be rendered are first parceled out across the network of available computers. The computers go to work and upon completion load the finished images onto videotape for viewing and critiquing the next morning.

Despite the low level of human participation in this final step, it is not without its difficulties. Sometimes the rendering code breaks down, and the person in charge must immediately solve the problem to avoid wasting valuable time. Unfortunately, with large animations running on several computers at once, finding the source of the problem is not always easy. How do you tell which machines are doing fine and which have crashed? The staff at Lamb & Company developed an amusing way to cope with this while working on *The Incredible Crash Dummies*. They gave each machine a voice. The computers that were working correctly sounded like cows grazing contentedly in a pasture, while any that had broken down shattered the mooing with the sound of breaking glass.

Facing page: Note the reflections, highlights, and shadows of the evil Junkman in his hideout in *The Incredible Crash Dummies*. (© 1993 Tyco Industries.)

Computer Animation Is Not Just for Cartoons

The usefulness of computer animation goes far beyond simply making better cartoons. Medical doctors now use it regularly to discover without surgery what is going on inside the human body. Astronomers create animations of newborn stars. And architects show new buildings to their clients before they are even built.

Facing page: Architects can create extremely realistic models to show their clients. *(Courtesy of Caligari Software.)*

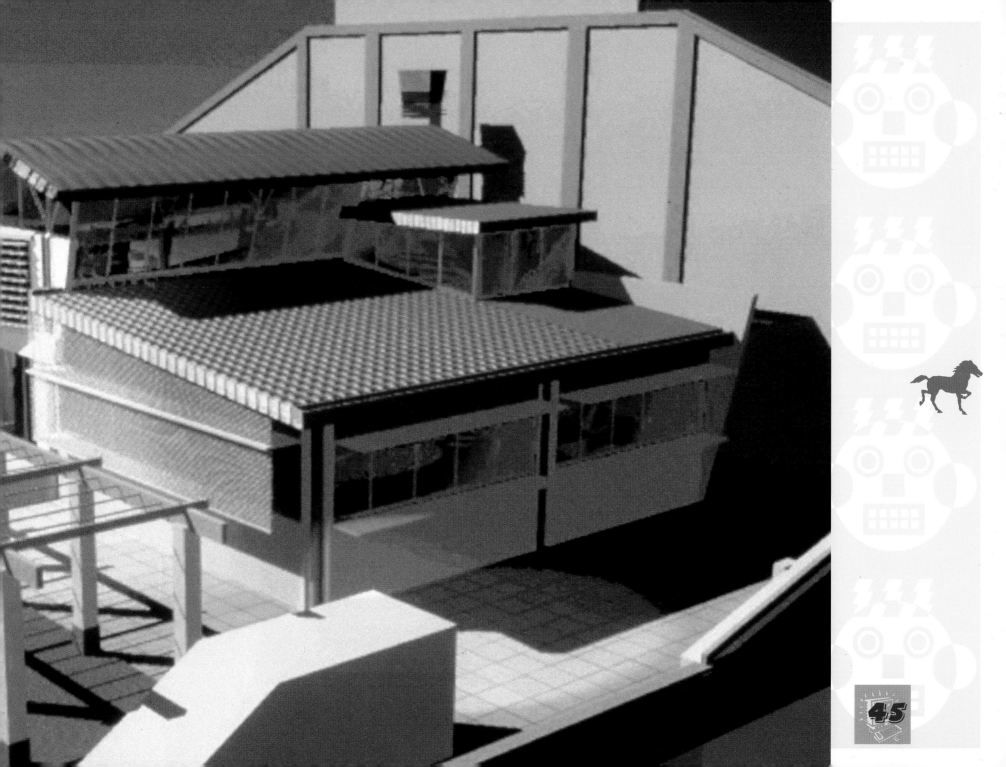

And in the entertainment field, even though computer animation has produced such smash hit films as Disney's *Toy Story*—the world's first 100 percent computer-animated feature film—its value does not stop with cartoons. It is the heart and soul of modern special effects. Among countless computer-created TV commercials, it has transformed automobiles into tigers for Exxon and brought the Pillsbury Doughboy to life. For the film industry, it has created the living dinosaurs of *Jurassic Park*, the chrome T1000 robot for *Terminator 2*, and the comical skeletons of *Toys*. In addition, it has been used in almost every film since 1994 in many behind-the-scenes tasks, such as erasing safety wires worn by actors in dangerous stunt scenes, and creating huge crowds by duplicating small groups of extras. Whatever the use, the computer has contributed immensely to the power of the stories being told.

This sequence shows the power of the computer technique called *morphing*. By mixing two images in the computer, a car driving along a desert road is transformed into a bounding tiger. *(Courtesy of Exxon Company, U.S.A., © Exxon Corp. 1995.)*

47

The Future

Woody the cowboy and Buzz Lightyear try to outdo each other in the Disney/Pixar blockbuster, *Toy Story*. (© 1996 Pixar/Disney. All rights reserved.)

Despite the incredible successes of computer animation, we have barely scratched the surface of its potential. Computer animation is going to change entertainment in countless ways. For one, it will make filmmaking more economical. This in itself will open the door for a new wave of films that might not otherwise be made. For another, it will change how we, the audience, are entertained. As interactive technologies, such as virtual reality and simulator rides, become more sophisticated, we will soon be able to play a part in a story and affect the outcome.

The potential for computer animation is so great, it's almost mind-boggling. Just as people who grew up with the horse and buggy couldn't imagine actually putting a man on the moon, we can't possibly see where the computer and its ability to draw pictures will take us. The possibilities are as limitless as our own imaginations, and it's all just a mouse-click away.

Index

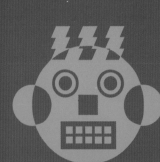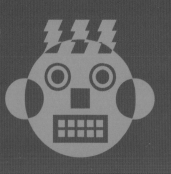

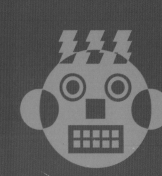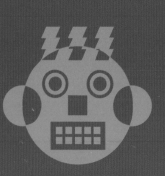